In the beginning, we are just seeds waiting to be planted. Seeds, in this case, that are female.

Somewhere between here and here it happens.

and so we can see that the specimen exhibit some signs of life — having lived fully, even (apparently) laughing heartily on several occasions

We become no longer young but not quite old. We become the dreaded phrase "A woman who has really lived."

We become ripe.

RIPE

the truth about growing older and
the beauty of getting on with your life

Janet Champ | Charlotte Moore

BEYOND
WORDS
Publishing
I N C

Beyond Words Publishing, Inc.
20827 N.W. Cornell Road, Suite 500
Hillsboro, Oregon 97124-9808
503-531-8700

The information contained in this book is intended to be inspirational,
not medical, and is in no way considered a replacement for consultation with
a duly licensed healthcare professional. The author and publisher are in no way
liable for any use or misuse of the information.

Managing editors: Sarabeth Blakey and Julie Steigerwaldt
Proofreader: Marvin Moore
Design and composition: Charlotte Moore

Printed in China

Library of Congress Cataloging-in-Publication Data

Champ, Janet.
    Ripe : the truth about growing older and the beauty of
getting on with your life / Janet Champ and Charlotte Moore.
        p. cm.
    1. Menopause—Popular works.   I. Moore, Charlotte.   II. Title.
RG186.C445   2005
618.1'75—dc22

                                                          2005009485

The corporate mission of Beyond Words Publishing, Inc.:
    Inspire to Integrity

This book is dedicated to our mothers.

LET'S OPEN THE DOOR
(A PREFACE)

Enough hiding in shame. Enough going it alone in the dark. This isn't a plague we're spreading. This isn't some disfiguring ailment that makes strangers run screaming into the hills or a criminal act we unwittingly commit. So let's bring it out into the open where it belongs.

IT IS, IT SEEMS, THE FINAL TABOO. The last gasp, the last hill we climb, the suddenly defining moment when our fertility and our femininity and our inherently following fantastic-ness wave bye-bye as into the valley we go.

Maybe some of us, the wise and the learned, the excruciatingly content and alarmingly sane, maybe we go skipping and strutting, thrilled to be part of the Great Big What Next waiting around the corner. And if this is you, and you've picked up this tome, please, stop sighing and keep reading. Because even with head held high, you may have hidden doubts. A nagging question. You may have friends (and you know who they are) who are not as content or confident and in need of, well, a conversation. A conversation with a book that does not snicker, a book that does not judge, a book that can be read with a flashlight if necessary like some million-member-outdoor-school-camp we're all in together. Someone, bring the S'mores.

Because, well, this:

Maybe some of us do not go happily. Maybe some of us go unwillingly, nervously, cautiously. Maybe some of us go kicking and screaming and flailing and denying and making up fabulous excuses along the way. Maybe some of us throw something. Maybe others only go in heels, exquisite makeup, something pink. Maybe a whole bunch of us, thousands really, millions actually, maybe we wonder and pause, look and stare, sit and wait— "Oh, I'll catch the next Menopause Train, you go right ahead"—until time and reality come and push us into the valley and over the hill. As if over the hill is such a horrible, nasty, obnoxious thing. As if this isn't another phase in a long line of phases we've already—thank you acne, thank you unrequited love—entered, lived through, and left.

Menopause.

Bummer.

—E, age 42

The word strikes fear into the hearts and breasts and vulnerable nether regions of most women, the vast majority of women, even intelligent, confident, bordering-on-superior women, and we know; we asked. But who can blame any of us? We're afraid of the dark, and face it, this is a dark place. Little light has shined here. No map has been drawn. This is the place no one books tour groups to, no one travels back from bearing T-shirts and coffee mugs. This is the land where we are forced to turn in that precious amount of "woman" we were given, and squandered, so carelessly. This is where we stop being us. Or do we?

Look: We're human and we evolve or we stop. We're women and we grow. From the moment of birth we mutate and change and it's never done, this process. Just look at your hands right now, this minute. When did they start to look like this? And why do we care so much?

This book is about ripening. About the changes that life and age and time do to us, do for us; about accepting some changes, screaming about others, letting go, fighting back. It's about the land we all must enter someday, if we're damned lucky, and a look at why we're so afraid of going where others before us have so brilliantly, wonderfully, beautifully tread. Here we spend half our lives wanting to be all grown up, mature. And then when we get there we cower and complain and want to go back.

And in the final, ending analysis there's one truth: If we can't accept ourselves for who and what we are, no one else can accept us either. So. Let's talk about what we don't want to talk about. Let's talk about what gives us shivers and goose bumps and hot flashes and cold spells in the middle of the night. What are we afraid of, anyway? A taboo is a taboo only because someone (Society maybe? Men maybe? Our mothers maybe? We love to blame our mothers) made it that way.

what makes a woman
feel — her youthful
with the benefit
after a certain point i

n a woman with her
low? Breasts held high
hands if this is true
aren't women at all.

What if this great endless valley before us is really more of an undiscovered paradise? A garden where once again we — aren't we lucky? — get to pick fruit from the Tree of Knowledge instead of the Tree of Benign Ignorance? It could be, it may be, that what we're headed for isn't the dark ages at all but something altogether lighter. Brighter.

Be. Not. Afraid.

Things may get a little messy. You may get a little messy. But that's the way it is meant to be. Life itself is messy and ripe, waiting to be picked rough skin and all. After all, it's not the end of the world. It's not even the end of your own private cul-de-sac.

It's the next chapter. The next beginning. It's the rest of your life. And lucky you: You get to live it.

[NOTE: FROM "ARGH" TO "ZIPPITY-OH-NO"

Let us now praise the handy euphemism. It rescues us in polite society. It adds complexity to our native tongue. It shelters us from all those vulgar terms considered harsh, blunt, offensive, realistic.

Being nothing if not eloquent, the female population of our planet has invented over one hundred words for menopause, most of them unprintable and involving elaborate body language. Odd, isn't it, that we have so many ways to say what we don't want to talk about? All these euphemisms and hardly a place to use them. That is, until now.]

37. THE SCARLET M

38. THE OVER-THE-HILL GANG

39. THE END OF LIFE AS WE KNOW IT

40. THE M WORD

41. THE M-M-M-M-M-M-M-M-M WORD

42. THE CHANGE

43. THE BIG CHANGE

44. THE LAST CHANGE UNTIL YOU KNOW WHAT

45. YOU KNOW, THAT THING THAT HAPPENS

46. THE DEATH OF MY FERTILITY

47. THE LAST OF MY EGGS

48. THE MOMENT MY MOTHER DENIES HAVING

49. THE LAST STAND

50. IT'S OVER, PERIOD (.)

51. THE OVER-AND-DONE-WITH GANG

52. WOMEN OF A CERTAIN AGE

53. WOMEN WHO HAVE BEEN THERE, DONE THAT

54. THE LAND THAT TIME FORGOT

55. THE VALLEY OF DARKNESS

56. THE VALLEY OF INFERTILITY

57. THE THING THAT HAPPENS WHEN YOU'RE OLD

58. THE MENOPAUSAL JUNGLE

59. THE ANTI-PUBERTY

60. PUBERTY IN REVERSE

61. THE CURSE OF THE FEMALE CLASS

62. A BANG AND THEN A WHIMPER

63. WHAT MY GRANDMOTHER HAD

CHAPTER 1
THE MORE WE CHANGE

Instead of changing and aging and watching it all pack its bags and move south, wouldn't it be nicer just to make time stand still? Oh come on, where's your sense of adventure? Then **you** would stand perfectly still too. And how dreary and mind-numbing and uninspiringly boring would that be?

THERE'S THIS MOMENT RIGHT BEFORE YOU GO TO THE DOCTOR when you feel the best you've felt in weeks, months, your entire known life. And the day you finally get in to cut/trim/color/all three your unruly, desperate locks only to look in the mirror and think *Today, my hair is the stuff of legend.* And all you want is to stop the clock, hold this moment, preserve it in amber, knowing that this, right here, is the best you'll ever be, ever look, ever breathe. Why, exactly, does it have to end?

The human part of us, the part that knows gravity on an intimate, first-name basis, it just wants to put its feet up and refuse alterations. But the eternal part of us, the part we can't quite diagnose or keep down, it goes on. This is the part that knows we're not done, not over, not through, and never will be.

Our bodies keep changing no matter how we tie them down, slam them shut, tell them to be quiet and behave. They, funny things, apparently don't want to stay 16 forever or take a twelve-year hiatus at 28; they don't wish to stay up *there* when they can hang about down *here*, they seem to look forward to the days of flesh sliding and settling and slipping and becoming, oh, something else entirely. Our bodies don't find this odd. Why do we?

Change is not only positive, it's vital. This is the part we don't concede to or conspire with, appreciate or acknowledge. This is where the plastic surgeons come in, rubbing palms. Where the gravity-despisers say, "Have I got something for you!" Where the lotions and the potions and the hope in a jar (a gallon, a fifty-ton drum) roll over to greet us and promise us the eternal life of an eternal life.

Things shift. Things fall. Things do a real slow fade. But our bodies, which have rhythms and ways we still haven't begun to read, let alone

A PRAYER

If this too (too) sullied flesh must fall,
please let it fall
in the most pleasing way possible.
Gravity is one nasty mother.

Amen.

conquer, know that it's necessary to slow down, yield, reach some sort of finish line. Without slowing down, life — and every road in it — is just a blur. To actually make out colors, patterns, a face in a crowd, we hit pause. Not stop, but pause. It's easy for any wag to say the moment we're born is the moment we start dying. But this is a pessimistic view of a pretty optimistic time. The moment we're born is when our bodies start living. And living, in every case, is where cells breathe and cells expire and flesh refuses to stay still or stagnant or dormant for too long.

Look: "Change is good for the soul" is a cliché because it's true. It's a cliché because the harder we kick and scream the more pathetic we become. And our throats, more hoarse.

And the alternative would be...?

Right. Let's get moving then, shall we?

[NOTE: FOR EVERYTHING WE GIVE UP WE GET IN RETURN. HEREWITH A LIST.

The things we lose:

☐ *our youth* ☐ *our periods* ☐ *our acne (please, God)* ☐ *our eggs* ☐ *our most outrageous expectations* ☐ *our most outrageous fears* ☐ *firm, lovely buttocks (if we had them in the first place)* ☐ *perky breasts (if they ever perked)* ☐ *skin that bounces back* ☐ *breasts that bounce back (see above)* ☐ *our ankles* ☐ *our knees* ☐ *tampons and the assorted accoutrements* ☐ *the fearlessness of a 16-year-old* ☐ *the naïveté of a 16-year-old* ☐ *our exasperation at not being taken seriously* ☐ *our memory, some of it* ☐ *our desire, some of it* ☐ *sleep* ☐ *fertility* ☐ *some glow, but not all* ☐ *some get up and go, but not all* ☐ *our nifty and fabulous metabolism* ☐ *believing that this moment, right now, is the most important thing in the world* ☐ *unrequited love that leaves us weeping in the night* ☐ *requited love that leaves us weeping in the day* ☐ *our supreme sense that we are always, always right* ☐ *self-loathing* ☐ *self-importance* ☐ *selfishness*

The things we gain:

☐ *our sense of confidence* ☐ *our sense of humor* ☐ *perspective* ☐ *wrinkles (laugh lines, crow's feet, worry lines, worry trenches, the roadmap of our life)* ☐ *class* ☐ *knowledge* ☐ *wit with the judicious use of sarcasm* ☐ *weight* ☐ *weight in the oddest places* ☐ *jowls, unfortunately* ☐ *neck skin, from where, exactly?* ☐ *never having to wonder if we have tampons* ☐ *tolerance* ☐ *understanding* ☐ *rational thought* ☐ *self-acceptance* ☐ *the persistent and radically interesting effects of gravity* ☐ *the art of letting go* ☐ *the art of giving back* ☐ *wisdom, whether we want it or not* ☐ *the art of self-deprecation* ☐ *the art of self-love* ☐ *compassion for the girl we used to be*

□ freedom]

WARNING: Objects may be closer than they appear. They may be whispering in your ear even now. Do not panic. Just hold the hand of the girl in front of you and walk single file. You are now entering...

CHAPTER 2
THE WARNING SIGNS AND
HOW TO READ THEM

WEBSTER'S ONLINE DICTIONARY DEFINES *menopause* with the following scientifically accurate sentences:

> The time in a woman's life when menstruation diminishes and ceases, usually between the ages of 45 and 50. Also called change of life.

That's the entire definition. *Meow, merchant,* and *merge* all enjoy longer, more interesting definitions, but menopause is somehow left with less to say, and more to imagine. It's correct. It's close, but very far away.

The thing that dictionaries and other sources we rely upon (be it friends, family, physicians, things we hear and books we read) may not tell us is that like most everything else in our lives, menopause is a distinctly individual process. Some of us experience symptoms others never face. Others experience symptoms they had no idea were indicative of menopause at all. Some of us start going through the menopausal motions (scientific name: *perimenopause*) very young, in our 30s. Others are well past 50. There are women, and there are millions of them, who enter menopause neither knowing they're experiencing it nor that their feelings, their "symptoms," are entirely expected, human, normal. And nothing to be ashamed of.

And there are women, and their name is legion, who reach a certain age and believe that they are literally going insane. Without laughter, without winking, without irony. Just a tremendous amount of confusion, and sometimes, despair. They feel, well, "different" is the only word for it, and why does different suddenly seem so scary? Same woman, same life, but something is akimbo. They can't sleep. Or they want to sleep all the time. They're anxious. Or worried. They're irritable, angry, cranky. They're depressed, ready to weep when the phone rings, ready to weep when it doesn't. They start forgetting why they walked into the kitchen. They start forgetting why it even matters.

And while some of these women may believe the disorder is all in their heads (I'm Really Not Myself Today), it's in their bodies, in their blood, and it's no disorder at all. It's the second great change of our female lives.

Menopause is the time of life when fertility ceases to exist. It's the time when the body doesn't have to worry about creation any longer; instead, it concerns itself only with existence. Our hormones, both estrogen and progesterone, decrease. Our menstruation cycles slow down, become erratic, eventually stop altogether. Our metabolism slows down or speeds up, allowing our normal physical responses (to heat, cold, pain, pleasure) to fluctuate. The process itself is evolutionary and complete. But the process is so personal that two friends may be going through menopause at the same time and show none of the same signs or conditions. Aggravating, sure. Enlightening, why not?

What follows are some warning signs, symptoms, feelings, things you might experience with menopause: *hot flashes, night sweats, heart palpitations, depression, insomnia, mood swings, loss of appetite, increased appetite, decreased sexual interest, increased sexual interest, interruptions/changes in your period, extreme fatigue, memory loss, forgetfulness, lack of enthusiasm, lack of interest in formerly interesting things (television shows you used to love, men you used to love, men you used to find attractive, women you used to find attractive, hilarious anecdotes, the future, the past, where you put your car keys, why you even drive, food, art, music, true love, blatant breaking-the-seven-deadly-sins-barrier lust, and so on).*

I am so sorry. I seem to be someone else today.

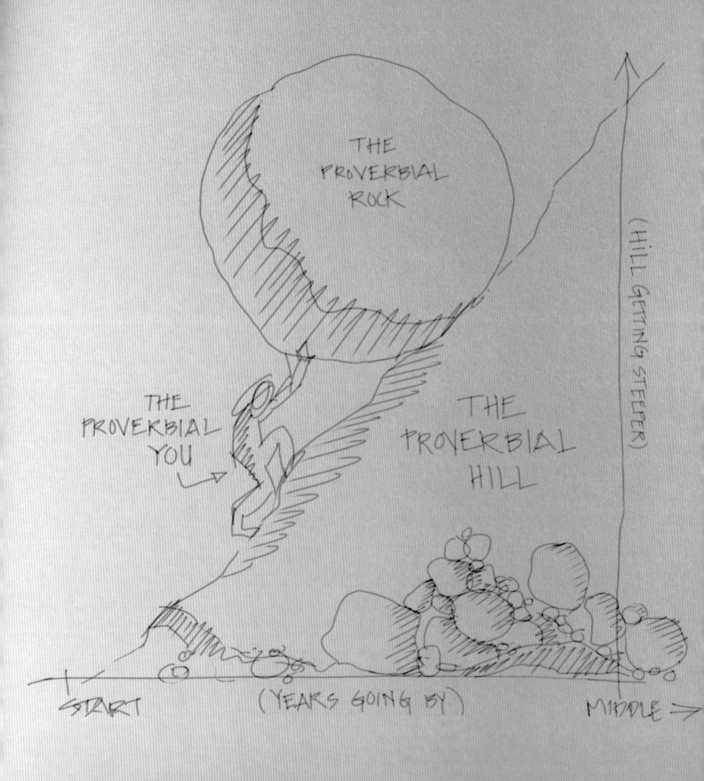

THE
PROVERBIAL
ROCK

(HILL GETTING STEEPER)

THE
PROVERBIAL
YOU

THE
PROVERBIAL
HILL

START   (YEARS GOING BY)   MIDDLE →

Warning signs come in as many flavors as women do. If in doubt, ask a doctor. If in doubt about your doctor, ask another. Suffer nothing without seeking an opinion, a treatment, an answer. This is your body and only you can read it. So read it well.

[NOTE: PERIMENOPAUSE AND WHAT IT IS/ISN'T

Perimenopause: The stage right before menopause occurs (the stage and its length vary according to each individual)

It's like this: Perimenopause is the beginning of the teeter. Menopause is the end of the totter. There's a start. And then a finish. There's a hill and a rock, and you're Sisyphus, and if you don't push that rock up the hill, the mess it will make is frightening. The truth is, perimenopause can last for ten years —ten years!— which means you can start having fluctuations in your cycle, in your hormonal balance, as early as age 20, and start experiencing menopause in your early 30s. We didn't say it was fair. We just said it was normal.

It's also like this: Perimenopause is not the end of the world as you know it. You're still fertile. You're still producing eggs, a menstrual cycle, both estrogen and progesterone. All it is, simply and truly, is a slowing down of the body's natural chemistries. Some biologists believe that the earlier puberty begins, the earlier perimenopause begins. Meaning, if you started puberty at age 11, you may enter perimenopause in your late 20s or 30s. Others think it has more to do with diet, heredity, and lifestyle. All we know is it's the foyer, the reception hall, to menopause. Please, après vous.]

CHAPTER 3

This all seems so familiar and yet so oddly, prepubescently wrong. Déjà you. Yes, in a way, you have been here before. Which is why you can call menopause...

THE ANTI-PUBERTY

OH, TO BE ELEVEN AGAIN. Or twelve or thirteen or fourteen or seventeen and a half if you were Mindy Kassenbaum and the teachers were beginning to get worried about you. There you were, contentedly stealing bases from the boys in softball or taking off Barbie's clothes and refusing to put them back on or climbing trees and refusing to come back down, or something, and then it hit you right between the eyes. Sometimes, quite literally.

The Hormonal Big Bang, the Krakatoa East (or perhaps it truly is West) of the preteen body, all the spewing and the churning and the shouting, some of it actually coming from us. This was the thing fifth-grade health class taught us, wasn't it? Why weren't we listening? The thing our mothers taught us (some with the seriousness of a philosopher, some with the embarrassed sigh of an oracle, some just putting a small pink pamphlet on our beds when we weren't looking, the one with all the nifty diagrams and callouts that made us both nervous and, well, nervous). The thing we all assumed was like turning a page, crossing a line, going from Mr. Thoma's history class to Ms. Rosenthal's English class right across the hall. Quick. Painless. Mundane.

Boy Oh Boy were we wrong. Because if all the world's a stage, puberty is Act 1 as written by Shakespeare, music by Wagner, adaptation by John Waters. It's the time when our bodies become physiologically capable of sexual reproduction, but the word is "capable" not "proficient" or "excelling" or even "prepared emotionally-not-to-mention-mentally" for that kind of event. Meaning our bodies go through hoops getting ready for the miracle of birth, but they have no intention of telling our hearts and minds and vivid imaginations about it. Here we become sexually mature in all sorts of palpable physical ways while still being, essentially,

**EVERYTHING
YOU NEED TO KNOW
NOW THAT
YOU'RE A WOMAN***

***OF A CERTAIN AGE**

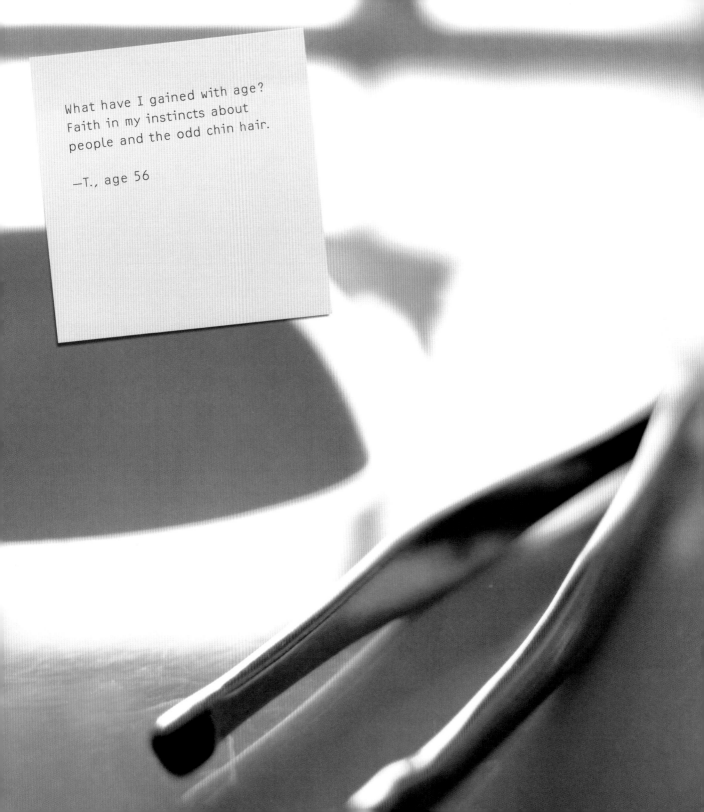

What have I gained with age?
Faith in my instincts about
people and the odd chin hair.

—T., age 56

children. One day we're playing foursquare or volleyball and the next day we've gone over an edge we didn't quite see coming.

We suddenly have breasts, but we don't yet know how to use them. (*Nor should we.*) Hair begins to appear in places we're fairly certain hair isn't supposed to be and we think *Tweezers? Shaving? Praying? Keeping the lights off? Calling in sick to P.E. for the next six years?* One day our baby-smooth skin has baby-sized bumps on it and these bumps don't go away, they erupt. We're greasy. We're moody. We're bitchy. We have thoughts about the third baseman that don't involve stealing, and above all of this we're confused, we're confused, we're confused.

And then just when we reach the age of real maturity, whatever divine numeral that may be, it happens all over again. What nature wound up at thirteen, nature now winds down. Here we thought we'd gone through all the crappy years, all the awkwardness and the blind dates and the pregnancy tests and the cramps and the birthing of babies and the burping of babies and the raising of babies and now we can just sit back and float down the River of Ahh, but no. We get more. We women, we who don't complain enough about enough, we get more.

All those hormones that went rushing through our bloodstreams decide it's time to slack off. Now that the body thinks there's no need to reproduce (it didn't ask us, did it?), it begins to shut the system down. Shut some things, that is, while keeping others positively blazing.

Like puberty, the side effects can be wild and varied and intense. Like puberty, it's hard to tell what's "normal" and what's not normal at all. And, like puberty, it's a trip that can feel decidedly lonely when there is no reason it should be. What it *should* be, is a celebration.

Because think what you can let go.

You can let your self-esteem out for a walk because you have nothing to prove, no one else you're supposed to be. You can have sex without worry of pregnancy. You can think of yourself instead of thinking constantly of the 12,134 (rough estimate) people you've ever met or known. You can blow off steam without apology because frankly, you've earned it.

See, the thing is this: If we can make it through puberty (and we did, didn't we?), we can make it through anything. If we could make it through unrequited love and crushes on our social studies teacher, stuffing our bras or pretending our bra's not even there; if we can make it through the high rises of acne and the lowdown on leg hair, we can make it through the other side of the hormonal coin. We cannot only survive but learn from it. Can't we? Really, can't we? Oh of course we can.

[NOTE: 14 v. 40

At 14 everything is so damn incredibly incurably oh-stop-the-world-I-want-everything-and-I-want-it-now important. We're obsessed with ourselves. We're obsessed with our hair our skin our teeth our breath our underarms our ankles our toes for god's sake our toes our smell our walk our talk our chances of being noticed and our chances of being noticed for all the wrong things. At 40 we don't care as much. If at all. At 40 we are starting to say Here I am, aren't I something? At 40 we are hitting the anti-puberty, the end of self-obsession and the beginning, girls, of self-possession. And yes, you can quote us.]

CHAPTER 4
LOVE & MENOPAUSE—A LETTER

TO ALL OUR SIGNIFICANT OTHERS: Maybe we do always hurt the ones we love. Maybe the maelstrom around us can't help but touch you, you who matter most, because you see us at our least guarded. Our most raw, real, true. And we know now that you go through menopause too, only the menopause you go through is ours. It's not a gift we intended to give; it's not a party we wanted you to join. But if you love us (and want to go on loving us) then it is a ride that comes gratis with the Roller Coaster That Is Us. This chapter is for you.

Dear You,

This thing that's happening -- it didn't creep up one sweaty, uncomfortable night as it might seem. It's been coming for years. And I'd like to say that it's all about me, and not about you, because in a way that's The Truth. But the fact is, even though it's happening inside me, it's happening to both of us. I'm changing. And that means that we may have to change too.

Just think of me as a funhouse mirror. I used to reflect you in a way that you liked. Now, well, maybe that reflection is a little funny looking. But it's still you. It's just that maybe you'll see yourself differently through me for a while.

You know. You've seen it coming too. Even though we didn't want to give it a name. The anger, sometimes explosive. The accusations. My need to press ahead with...well, I hate to repeat words so soon in what promises to be a long letter but...with my needs.

You see, suddenly, my needs, me, I -- we -- are all out front. You and I have been together a long, long time, and you've been very good to me, but there are things I need to attend to, and I'm not sure I can let anything or anyone get in the way. It shouldn't harm you, or us. We should get through this just fine if...

...if you can manage to see that this is about me really becoming myself. I've had a whole lifetime to grow in the womb. Now it's time for me to be born.

Me. The first two letters of menopause. (Funny how that works out, isn't it? "Men" is the first three letters, but I'm afraid "men" come second. "Me" comes first. You'll just have to sit in the passenger seat

for a while, and buckle your seat belt, because it may
be a bumpy ride.

Maybe I'll seem crazy to you. Really crazy. And
though I've always been super articulate about how I
feel (and have, in fact, criticized you for sometimes
being unable to express clearly how you feel, and now
I'm really really sorry about that), I'm not necessar-
ily going to be able to do it anymore myself. Looks
like we're going to trade places for a while. My moods
and feelings are going to elude my own powers of recognition and explanation. I won't know why I'm angry
or sad or nervous. I'll just feel that way, because
that's how I'm going to feel. And you'll just have to
let me feel that without pressing me to explain or
saying that thing you always say when you're trying to
help: "What do you want me to do about it?" I won't
want you to do anything about it. I'll just want you
to understand.

(Understand?)

Sometimes I'm going to seem really -- and here's
that word again (and I hate this word) -- needy. I'll
need to know that you still love me. That after all
these years, I'm still your woman.

That said, I'm not always going to want to be
with you. Oh, ha ha, the irony! I may want to be
alone. A lot. I may not be interested in sex for a
while. Who knows? Maybe I'll be a raging nympho-
maniac (that would be nice). I may not want to be
touched. Or I may want to be wrapped forever in your
arms. We'll just have to wait and see.

This is scary. Wait, is this scary?

No. Let's not be scared. People, and I don't
mean women, I mean men and women, have been going

through this forever. Right? Right. I mean, what
is all of this if not just another phase, another
part, no, another opportunity. Like I said before,
another birth.

I know, I know. Sometimes the metaphorical talk
works and sometimes it's irritating. OK, this is what
I mean: I want my life to be about growth, not about
getting old. I want it to be about moving forward with
courage and creativity and reinvention if necessary.
Not about cowering and stopping and stooping and
hiding behind a closed door. This will be hard for you
too. But you know what? I do love you. And I want you
to know that today and every day of our lives
together.

And one more thing. If you need to change, if you
need things to be about you instead of me for a while
-- a whole decade even -- I'll let you do that. If you
need to feel uncertain and scared, and you can't tell
me why...if you need to be alone or together or
silently alone together, I'll let you do that. If you
need to rage, I'll let you rage. And I'll try not to
do anything -- especially not get in your way -- but
understand.

When we are done with menopause, you and me, we
will have changed for the better. You'll see.

Love,
Me

[DISCLAIMER: NO WOMAN IS AN ISLAND, NOT EVEN IBIZA

In the next few weeks and months and years there may be times when, try as you might, the shrapnel flares and someone gets wounded. Could be anyone: your friends, your employees, your trying-to-do-her-best mother, your completely uncomprehending father, your younger and perkier sister, the latte girl you just bitched at without meaning to, your children, your children's friends, the complete strangers who unintentionally cross your path, your dog. This isn't, however, justification for bad behavior. The words "I'm sorry, I'm having a tough time right now" can lead to understanding, which leads to empathy, which leads to group hugs and chocolate. Ah yes, there's an upside to everything.]

THE NOWOMANISAN ISLAND BRIDGE PROJECT:

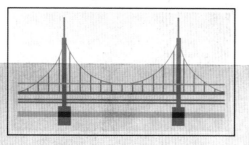

Proposed

East and West

Construction

Sites

Santa Sorella

SISTERHOOD

Fallopian

Strait

M

Gulf of Unders

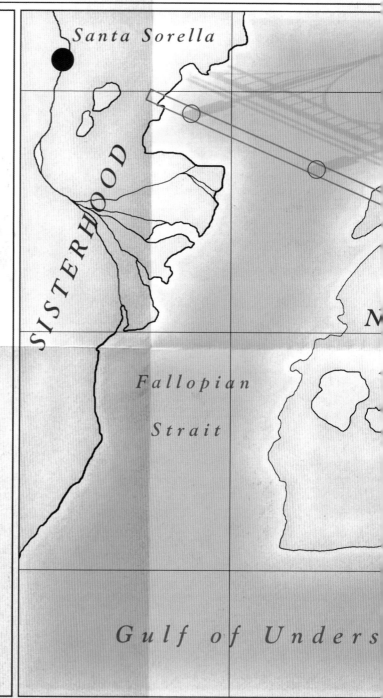

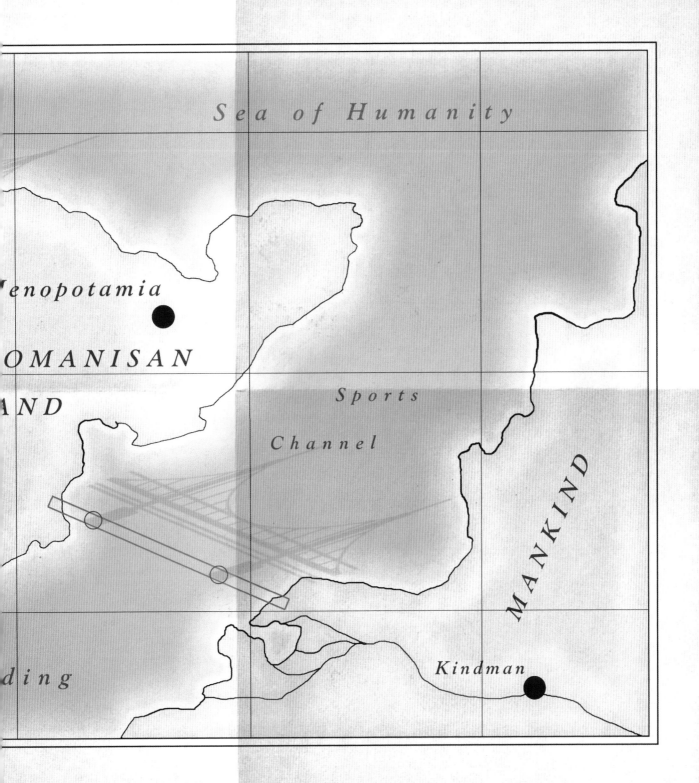

[NOTE: MEN GET MENOPAUSE TOO

Men get menopause too. So what is male menopause? (Fascinating scientific term: andropause.*) That's easy. It's the panic attack you get when somebody younger, hairier, or smoother saunters in and gets your promotion. It's the slap in the face when you look in the mirror and see not only dear old dad but dear granddad. It's when sports cars start looking not only affordable but compulsory. It's all the stuff that comes rushing over you, unasked and unwanted. Like random erectile dysfunction or impotence. Pattern baldness. Intricate prostrate exams. Wrinkles that have nothing to do with character. Lack of interest, lack of desire, lack of pretty much everything that used to come so easily. Put them all together and you have something approximating menopause. Yes, you can go lie down now.*]

"Sorry."

"Stop! I want to get off!"

CHAPTER 5
WOMAN, HEAL THYSELF

The ancient Greeks believed that the moon influenced not only the tides of earthly oceans but the menstrual and menopausal tides of the female body as well. Menopause = "Moon stop." So our own private satellites may wind down, but we go on. The good news: We have our choices. These are some of them...

HERE YOU HAVE THE HONEST TRUTH: Your body is in your hands. (Please, don't drop it.) Our bodies belong, flesh and blood and everything in between, to us. By way of connection they also belong to those who love us and do not want to see us miserable or unwell. So it's not enough to sit back and let age have its way with us without even putting up a fight. Because if these bodies belong to us, they are our responsibility, our liability. Do we eat what's good for us instead of merely gratifying? Do we appreciate our skin and bones for what they still can do, or do we reprimand them for what they can no longer achieve? Can we still distinguish our flesh from the fabric of the couch, or have they melded into something harmonious? In other words, do we take care of ourselves, or are we hoping someone else will jump up and do it for us?

Because they won't, you know. Very seldom does that knock on the door, that remedy tied with a pretty bow, arrive with our names on it. Listen: If we can take care of others so damn well, we can take care of ourselves. Herewith, a list of symptoms that come with the banquet that is menopause, and some suggestions of remedies that may help, heal, contain, relieve, and give respite.*

OK then. Now that we have your attention, the menu, please.

*Let's think before we put anything in our body or on our body or anywhere within a fifty-mile radius of our body. We are not guinea pigs. Most of us have never even been to Guinea. So let's get all the hormone-replacement facts and figures out of the closet and into the streets where they belong, and see what works, what hinders, what protects.

WELCOME TO

THE MOON STOP CAFE

WHERE IT'S ALWAYS HOT, FRESH, AND INDIVIDUALLY PACKAGED.
AND WHERE THE CHOICE IS ALWAYS UP TO YOU.
PICK ONE, PICK ALL, EAT AS IF YOUR LIFE DEPENDED ON IT.
(AND PLEASE, TIP GENEROUSLY!)

THE MENU

INTRODUCTION

First, the details: Menopause is the end of menstruation as we know it. Our ovaries stop producing eggs, and the levels of female hormones, such as estrogen and progesterone, gradually diminish, although never disappear completely. Usually occurs between 45 and 55, could be earlier and could be later. Roughly 50 percent of all women never experience any symptoms. But that means 50 percent do.

FIRST COURSE: HOT FLASHES

Probably the most common symptom of menopause, hot flashes are apparently caused by changes in circulation and can occur several times a day (as many as 20 or more) and last for up to five minutes at a time. For many, these are simply irritating; for some, they are exhausting, embarrassing, and physically draining. Stress, alcohol, and tight clothing can all make hot flashes worse.

LAYER "CAKE" . . . . $
Many women find it easier to layer clothes, always being able to take off and put back on.

BREATHE EASY . . . . $
Slowing your breathing at the onset of a hot flash can help minimize it.

SHAKE A LEG . . . . $
Exercise can help reduce frequency.

GIVE ME AN "E" . . . . $
Vitamin E supplements may help with circulation and body temperature.

BLACK COHOSH B'GOSH . . . . $
Herbs such as black cohosh have been used for centuries to help minimize hot flashes. Most researchers believe black cohosh is able to diminish the levels of the luteinizing hormone that becomes elevated during menopause.

ME SOY HAPPY . . . . $
Soy isoflavins (which contain natural phytoestrogens*) have helped calm hot flashes and reduce their frequency.

SECOND COURSE: MOOD SWINGS, DEPRESSION, HIGH ANXIETY (AS WELL AS LOW AND MEDIUM), NERVOUSNESS

TAKE CONTROL . . . . $
If you feel out of control, try bringing control back. Yoga works for some women. For others, meditation.

HERBAL PLANNING . . . . $
Many women have found help by taking kava, a centuries-old remedy for anxiety and sleep-lessness. Other herbs that have shown some effect include valerian root, St. John's wort, and passion flower.

MOO . . . . $
Warm milk (including soy and rice), that mainstay of old black-and-white TV shows, has been proven to both relax and mildly sedate, as has hot cocoa.

VITAMINS TO THE RESCUE . . . . $
Vitamin E supplements may help with circulation and body temperature.

PINS 'N' NEEDLES . . . . $
Acupuncture may help reduce anxiety and depression.

UNDERSTANDING . . . . $
Understanding your fears and apprehension—addressing them instead of avoiding them—can lower stress as well. Talk to someone who may be going through the same thing.

THIRD COURSE: NIGHT SWEATS

The meaner, uglier sister of hot flashes. Night sweats come and eventually go, but they can leave behind insomnia, frequent sleep disturbance, restlessness, depression, anxiety, and sheets that are soaked before you can wash them.

DON'T EVEN GO THERE . . . . $
Try avoiding caffeine and alcohol in the evening. Try dong quai, chickweed, chaste berry, and licorice root instead.

SHAKE ANOTHER LEG . . . . $
Exercise at least three times a week to raise endorphins and reduce stress.

BATH NOW/SLEEP LATER..$

Wait half an hour or more after a hot bath before attempting sleep; this can help the body to regulate its temperature.

SLEEP EASY..$

Sleep in the nude. Sleep in comfortable, loose cotton. Sleep with a fan on. If you start tossing and turning, get up, read something boring, and only go back to bed when you're actually, truly tired.

SIDE ORDERS: HEADACHES

Less caffeine, less alcohol. Meditation, yoga, relaxation techniques all help. Exercise can increase circulation, lessening head pain. Many herbs have calming influences: chamomile, elderflower, sage, valerian, black cohosh, wild yam. Magnesium and vitamin B6 may help.

DESSERT: SEX YES/SEX NO

Decreasing estrogen can unfortunately play havoc with our sex lives. Desire and satisfaction can both be affected before, during, and after menopause. And as estrogen naturally decreases, the vagina can become thinner, drier, and shorter, making sex uncomfortable or difficult.

TALK: PART I...$

Talk to a doctor. Talk to a naturopath. Talk to your partner.

I LUBE YOU...$

Consider various lubricants. Consider taking red clover extract (in pill form or as a tea), which according to research helps relieve vaginal dryness. Try relaxation techniques to help nervousness. Borage oil, evening primrose oil, and flaxseed oil will give your body some of the essential fatty acids it needs, good for your skin both outside and in.

TALK: THE SEQUEL..$

Talk to your partner again. Ask for more foreplay, more hand-holding, more romance, more dirty words, whatever you need to make you (and your body) feel more comfortable and more desirous of sex itself.

SEXUAL HEALING..$

Remember that frequent sexual activity actually helps preserve the lining of the vagina and protects against infections, so there is good reason to persevere besides the actual Yowza factor.

CHEF'S REMEDY DU JOUR AND EVERY JOUR

Diet

What we eat is truly what we are. Eat less fat. Eat less processed, pre-packed foods. Eat a diet high in grains and fiber and vegetables and legumes. Cut down on processed sugar. Consume less caffeine or cut it out entirely. Look for phytoestrogens* that occur naturally in all sorts of foods: in fruit, especially apples, grapes, strawberries, pears, plums, oranges, pineapple, lemons and limes; in soy milk, soybeans, tofu, miso, many varieties of beans; in lentils, peas, flaxseed, many vegetables, an entire plethora of foods that can see us through many a physical (mental, emotional) trial. And foods to maybe avoid? Spicy food bothers some women, elevating their body temperatures, as do alcohol and caffeine.

Exercise

We are also what we do. Our bodies have a great capacity to remember. They are attuned to our fluctuations and our natural rhythms. Exercise often and regularly. Exercise whether you want to or not. Exercise to help not only your body but your mood, your emotions, your future. Walk if you cannot run, lift weights if you cannot walk, try aerobics, Pilates, swimming, yoga, something. The body remembers even if we forget.

A NOTE FROM OUR CHEF

Talk, look, listen, read, research, keep your mind and your ears as alive and open as your body. And always talk to a healthcare professional or doctor before attempting long-term remedies yourself.

*Phytoestrogens are estrogen-like compounds that mimic natural hormonal estrogen in our bodies. They help modulate the fluctuations that can cause hot flashes, night sweats, and other symptoms of menopause.

$ = ARE YOU KIDDING? RELIEF HAS NO PRICE.

It's your movie. You're the producer, the director, the cameraman, the best supporting actress (emphasis on "supporting"), and the leading lady. But drat, you have to write the script. So take a blank piece of paper and start typing...

CHAPTER 6
A DIALOG WITH YOURSELF

ME, THE MOVIE

INT. BATHROOM. EARLY-MORNING HOURS

A MEDICINE CABINET MIRROR reveals the tile wall before it. Sounds of WATER pouring from a faucet fill the room as steam rises in the air. A WOMAN'S head lifts up from the sink below and she stands, staring into the mirror with an expression that could easily be read as "Now What?" Her FACE, still wet from the washing, is completely unadorned. SHE leans in, examines her face closely, finds what she's looking for, and exhales in derision.

> SHE
> What's that? That's new. That wasn't around yesterday.

SHE turns and examines the right side of her face.

> SHE
> And oh goody. There's a matching one over here. Identical twins! My wrinkles are now starting to give birth to each other. How lovely. Soon, sextuplets.

Her inner voice decides to join in the monologue.

> HER
> Could be worse.

> SHE
> Seriously, I'm like a tree: you can count my age by the rings on my neck. How could it be worse? My wrinkles could get together and form a subway map? Someone could tell the Green line from the Blue just by reading my forehead?

                    HER
You're healthy. You're not decrepit.
You're smart, you're witty, you're
attractive, you don't look a day over
53.

                    SHE
I'm 52.

                    HER
Whatever. The point is your age is all
in your head. Not under your eyes, not
around your mouth, but your head. If
you were truly paying attention you'd
see what's gotten infinitely better
instead of worse. And come on, you're
a thousand times happier than you used
to be.

                    SHE
You come on. Says who? Says when?

                    HER
How about 11 through 16, when you were
certain you'd never date, never have
breasts, never be the head cheerleader,
never find the cure for the endless
human plague that is acne.

                    SHE
But I did have a 4.0. So there's that.

SHE takes a towel and wipes the gathering steam from the mirror.

                    HER
Or the fabulously stable ages of 16 to 22

I was dewy and everything was easy···

when you dated and lusted, lusted and
wept, fell in love forever until you
changed your mind five minutes later,
gave the nice boys a cold shoulder and
the bad boys both shoulders at once,
and very warmly I might add.

                    SHE
But at least I was young! I was dewy and
everything was easy and new and full of
possibility. Now everything is...done.
Over. Old. Blah.

                    HER
Oh bullshit.

SHE jumps back from the mirror as if she's been hit.

                    HER
Really, I cry bullshit. Life wasn't
easy then. Nothing was easy then.
That's just another convenient myth
we wrap around ourselves for comfort,
one that goes hand-in-hand with Yes I
Can Do It All! and Everyone Else Is
So Much Better Than Me.

                    SHE
What if they're not myths? What if
they're true and completely attain-
able...the brass ring at the end of the
rainbow.

                    HER
Keep mixing your metaphors and I'm shut-
ting up.

                              SHE
          Listen: Just because I can't do it all
          doesn't mean it isn't being done. Just
          because I can't be fifteen places at once,
          supermother and superwife and super-
          organization-queen doesn't mean it's
          not possible. Maybe it's just me. Maybe
          I'm the myth.

                              HER
          Maybe you're too hard on yourself.

                              SHE
          Maybe I'm not hard enough.

HER winces, sighs, and then speaks in almost a whisper.

                              HER
          Why do you expect so much?

                              SHE
          Why does everyone else expect even more?

THE FACE IN THE MIRROR isn't at all sure what to say.

                              HER
          ...OK. Valid question. Good question.
          The question of the Ages. But the ques-
          tion can be answered like this: I'm
          being myself as well as I can. As good
          and productive and human as possible.
          And isn't that enough?

                              SHE
          You tell me: Is it?

                              HER
               God you're aggravating. Don't get all
               Socratic on me now.

SHE is no longer listening but thinking of the life behind
her.

                              SHE
               Productive at what? What have I been
               productive at? Good at?

                              HER
               Being in love with the same person for 23
               years, for one. Living with instead of
               without. Staying when it would be easier
               to go. Making it through thick and thin
               and thinner than that. Raising a fam-
               ily that's relatively sane and healthy
               and interesting, for two. Taking care of
               infants who became children who became
               teenagers who became viable members of
               the real world and still call home without
               needing money, you might add that, too.

SHE brushes her hair -- with gusto -- as she goes on.

                              SHE
               OK, so there's that.

                              HER
               Having a job that becomes a career.
               Watching as it careens close to devour-
               ing your life, all-consuming and all-
               important, and then stepping back and
               making it what you're good at, what you

do instead of who you are. There's that,
too.

> SHE
> Well. I suppose so. Yes.

> HER
> Women you're still friends with, men
> you're still friends with, dogs and cats
> and various neighborhood pets who find
> you no less than thrilling. Doing a
> dozen things at once without applause
> or comment, throwing balls in the air
> and trying to balance them on the tip of
> your rather petite nose without any one
> noticing including, apparently, you.

> SHE
> We all do it.

> HER
> Yes, we all do it. And we are the only
> ones who can say enough. It. Is. Enough.

> SHE
> So I'm not a complete disappointment.

HER, trying not to be annoyed and wiping the mist on the
glass from her own looking-glass side.

> HER
> Not as far as I can tell. And besides.
> Remember when you were 18? You just
> wanted to be 21.

SHE, nodding her head now, remembering.

                         SHE
          And at 23 I just wanted to be 25.

                          HER
          And by 29 you already felt 30 so who
          cared?

                         SHE
          I wanted to be a woman, not a girl.

                          HER
          And so you are.

                         SHE
          But...I'm...the question is, what I need
          to know is: Am I still viable? Desir-
          able? Am I old or just older? Am I still
          me, whoever I was?

SHE turns on the light and looks at herself closely in
the mirror. She lifts her chin. She narrows her eyes. She
smiles.

                          HER
          Are you kidding? You're the most beau-
          tiful woman in the room.

SHE looks at herself one last time, satisfied with the face,
the person, in the mirror. Out loud she murmurs one last
thing.

                         SHE
          Then I guess I am.

SHE turns the LIGHT off as if blowing out a candle and leaves
the room, bathroom mirror and all.

Are you kidding
won

ou're the most beautiful
in the room.

hair and ma

H

second

H

tal

H

c

KITCHEN REFRIGERATO

mirro

MIRROR, MIR

FILMED ENT

NO ANIMALS OR STUNT DOUBLES

ANY RESEMBLANCE TO AC
PLACES, THINGS, CIRCUM
IS COMPLETELY A

for Herself
LF

director
LF

out
LF

g
, OCCASIONALLY, OVEN

lded by
PRODUCTIONS

ON LOCATION

HURT IN THE MAKING OF THIS FILM

PERSONS LIVING OR DEAD,
ES, EPISODES, OR EVENTS
TERLY INTENTIONAL

CHAPTER 7
ANY QUESTIONS? GOOD

"Hello students. My name is Ms. Betty Thomas and I will be your teacher for today." So there you were in seventh grade health class avidly listening or, more likely, avidly drawing concentric circles around your name on your gloriously grafitti-fied Peechee when the word "menopause" didn't come up. Why should it? That was a thousand years away. Some post-historic world you didn't have to sweat about. Well class, please be seated. And let the sweat begin.

THIS IS A TEST

Please use a number two pencil. Do not copy from your neighbor.
Do not copy from your neighbor's neighbor, relative, best friend,
acquaintance, or intimate stranger. Keep your eyes on your own
page. If in doubt, guess. If still in doubt, look at your neighbor.

SAMPLE:

Ⓐ Ⓑ Ⓒ ● Funny, but at my age, I suddenly seem more
attractive than ever before to:

    a. myself
    b. my dog
    c. younger men
    d. all of the above

When giving your answer, fill in the circles clearly and completely.

SAMPLES:

Ⓐ Ⓑ Ⓒ ◑   Ⓐ Ⓑ Ⓒ ⊗   Ⓐ Ⓑ Ⓒ ●
NO   NO   YES

If you have read and thoroughly understand these instructions,
please TURN THE PAGE AND BEGIN.

Getting older is:

a. a joke

b. the crime of the century

c. punishment for living this long

d. the gravy

In menopause your eggs actually:

a. start turning into chickens
b. completely stop producing
c. make an exquisite omelet
d. take up knitting

Most studies say up to 65 percent of women have menopausal symptoms that interrupt their normal lives. Which means a "normal" life is one without an abundance of (choose three):

a. hot flashes that come out of nowhere
b. night sweats that interrupt your sleep
c. anxiety, nervousness, and irrational mood swings that interrupt your daily life
d. ankle hair

One hundred percent (that's 100% to our mathematically inclined friends) say that emotional isolation might not only increase negative symptoms, it can also bring them on in the first place. So women can greatly reduce all this with the help of:

a. tapioca pudding
b. four or five Jude Law films followed by a martini chaser
c. supportive friends and family who listen and care
d. large crowds

Unfortunately, one of the things decreased estrogen levels gives older women in record numbers is osteoporosis, and there's nothing funny about it. Osteoporosis is caused by lack of calcium, and lack of our bodies to process the calcium we do get. Which is why women especially need to watch:

a. what we eat AND how much we eat
b. how much we move AND how much we stay sedentary
c. how much calcium and vitamin D we get every single day
d. all the above, please

Our vaginas do not only have monologues, they have continuing dialogs. They tell us, usually without the use of normal speech, things we might not want to listen to. Because even though we are ripe, our ripeness sometimes needs a little tender loving care. Because suddenly we notice our vaginas:

a. buying sports cars and dating much younger men
b. refusing to come out and play
c. needing a little more—what's the word?—juice*
d. looking way too much like Ethel Merman

*So sorry but so true: As we age, our skin, all of it, begins to lose moisture. So consider some over-the-counter lubrication if you notice sexual discomfort, or pain, or irritation. Don't be embarrassed. Don't think you're abnormal or hide or just stop having sex, because then you may feel more emotionally isolated than ever. Think of it as oil for the engine. Or for our domestic goddess friends, butter for the pan.

Wrinkles are Mother Nature's way of saying:

a. gotcha
b. life is unfair, unfunny, and unfortunately, unbearable
c. the more years we live the more our skin loses collagen and elasticity; it's a fact, not a sin
d. I control the horizontal, I control the vertical, and you never can predict the weather so don't even try

Gray hair is a sign of:

a.   sorrow

b.   pity

c.   beauty

d.   the cross

People who think all women over 40 are somehow less interesting, less attractive, less exciting, less desirable, less powerful, less important, less enticing, less anything are:

a. stupid
b. ignorant
c. unworthy of your company
d. to be pitied

Menopause is literally that special time when:

a. you haven't had a period for twelve straight months
b. you run naked in the streets and nobody notices
c. you get your first, or perhaps second, nipple ring
d. you turn to stone

The worst number in the world is:

a. 40
b. 50
c. 60
d. any number not followed by another number

Throughout the ages, human beings have created and honored—and archaeologists have discovered—hundreds of fertility goddesses. But so far archaeologists have found no "infertility goddesses" whatsoever. Why?

a. they're not concentrating hard enough
b. infertility just wasn't appreciated enough
c. fertility apparently had something to do with continuation of the species
d. trust us, it's the new black

With all the glorious women in the world over 40, over 50, over 70, over 80, I have to say my role model for growing old will be:

a. all the glorious women who have gone before
b. me
c. (a) and (b)
d. (b) and (a)

Let's not, this one time, give ourselves up for judgment. We're so tired, frankly, of fitting in with the expectations of others. Of a society that's always holding up standards we can't possibly meet. Give us something to reach for, to achieve— terrific. Ask us to try harder, to look beyond our own preconceptions, our personal bias—absolutely. But tear us down if we can't live up to an ideal of perfection—forget it.

So don't, just this once, judge even yourself. Unless you're willing to choose the grade you actually deserve.]

CHAPTER 8
WOMEN WE LOVE

MADELEINE ALBRIGHT MAYA ANGELOU SUSAN B.

ANTHONY MARGARET ATWOOD

JOSEPHINE

BAKER LUCILLE BALL

LAURIE ANDERSON GAI AULENTI

BRIGITTE BARDOT SIMONE DE BEAUVOIR

INGRID BERGMAN JANE BIRKIN

BARBARA BOXER LOUISE BOURGEOIS

A. S. BYATT ANNE CARSON

RACHEL CARSON ROSALYN CARTER JULIA

CHILD SHIRLEY CHISHOLM

RUBY

MARION CUNNINGHAM BETTE DAVIS

DEE DAME JUDI DENCH

RAY

EAMES SHIRIN EBADI

CATHERINE DENEUVE ISAK DINESEN

EVE ENSLER MARIANNE FAITHFUL ORIANNA

FALLACI DIANE FEINSTEIN M. F. K. FISHER

MARGOT

FONTEYN ELLEN GILCHRIST JANE GOODALL

ELLA FITZGERALD RUTH GORDON

KATHERINE GRAHAM MARTHA GRAHAM OUR GRANDMOTHERS GERMAINE

GREER PAM GRIER PEGGY GUGGENHEIM MARGHERITA HACK ZAHA

HADID

HEPBURN

DEBORAH HARRY

ARIANNA HUFFINGTON

MARCELLA HAZEN

EDITH HEAD

KATHERINE HEPBURN

MOTHER JONES

AUDREY

LENA HORNE

PATRICIA HIGHSMITH

REI KAWAKUBO

KING

CORETTA SCOTT KING

ROSE LEE

BILLY JEAN

DOROTHEA LANGE

EARTHA KITT

RITA LEVI-MONTALCINI

HELEN LEVITT

GYPSY

SOPHIA LOREN

DORIS LESSING

CLARE BOOTH LUCE

MARIAN MCPARTLAND

LORETTA LYNN

MARGARET MEAD

ELAINE MAY

AGNES DE MILLE

GOLDA MEIR

MINA

RITA

HELEN MIRREN

MARY TYLER MOORE

JEANNE MOREAU

MORENO

TONI MORRISON

IRIS MURDOCH

MARTINA

OUR MOTHERS

NAVRATILOVA

INGRID NEWKIRK

GEORGIA O'KEEFE

ANAIS NIN

JACQUELINE

KENNEDY ONASSIS

YOKO ONO

CAMILLE PAGLIA

ROSA

GRACE PALEY

PARKS

LYNN REDGRAVE

VANESSA REDGRAVE

JEAN RHYS

DAME

DIANA RIGG   ANITA RODDICK   ELEANOR ROOSEVELT   ISABELLA ROSSELLINI

GENA ROWLANDS   GEORGE SAND   MARGARET SANGER   CINDY SHERMAN

BEVERLY SILLS   NINA SIMONE   LIZ SMITH   MAGGIE SMITH   PATTI SMITH

SUSAN SONTAG   IMELDA STAUNTON   GERTRUDE STEIN   GLORIA STEINEM

TWYLA THARP   HELEN THOMAS   AGNÈS VARDA   DIANA VREELAND

ALICE WATERS   MAXINE WATERS   VIVIENNE WESTWOOD   JOANNE WOODWARD

(AND THE LIST, LIKE THEM, GOES ON.)

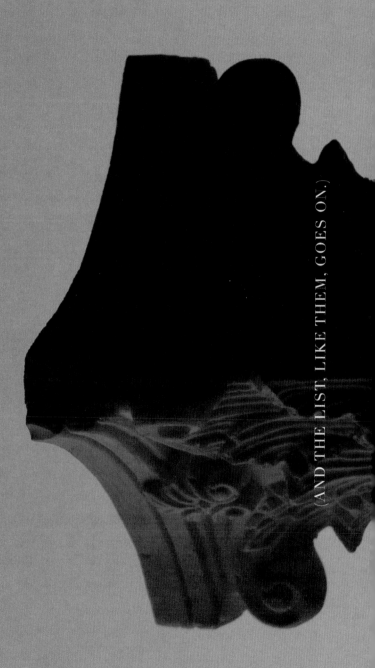

Maybe it's the way they thumbed noses both petite and large at limitations and expectations. Maybe it's because at age (put any multiple of ten here) they were just getting started. Maybe it's because to them age was as unimportant as gender, and gender was simply a birthright. Maybe it's simply that we flatter ourselves by thinking we could somehow, someday, be like them. This world of ours doesn't hold older women up in praise anymore, give them pedestals to stand on instead of lie beneath. But they're out there. It's our own fault if we choose not to see them. If we think them invisible. Each one an instance of age made meaningless—no, that's wrong—age made meaning**ful**. Each one worthy of a little adoration, much applause. Each one proving by any means necessary that the older we get, the riper we become.

CHAPTER 9
YOU ARE NOT ALONE
(EVEN THOUGH YOU COULD SOMETIMES SWEAR IN THE DARKNESS OF THE NIGHT THAT YOU ARE)

Herewith, some words of wit, wisdom, and commiseration from those who are entering into, ensconced in, or exiting from the forests and fields of Menopause Land. If you visit, be sure to write.

Even though the worst is over for me, I still feel anger and resentment that a woman is made to feel ostracized, a freak, a hysterical (horrible word) "loon." It's a very lonely experience and shouldn't be. —A., age 58

It was just one of those things that was never, ever discussed although one knew it was there... odd really, as every woman goes through it. —L., age 47

...a personal tsur

My Mom had some night sweats but reasoned to herself, "Maybe I shouldn't have had that second scotch." —S., age 58

I accord it the same importance I would the flu. You know you'll get it eventually but you know you'll get over it too. —T., age 52

Menopause? Let me put it like this. The really awful thing was being 13 and starting my periods. I could NOT believe I was going to have to endure that ordeal for the next 30 years. —A., age 72

I loved my period, cramps and all...bring it on...so beautiful and feminine...and I've been in mourning since it stopped 16 months ago. —S., age 46

My vision ar changed. O other is wor

age 54

Menopause was just another learning curve, challenge to rise to really. Depressing at first...but like time...it marches on and you deal with it. —M., age 49

Maybe I'll rid myself of migraines, if I'm not having monthly psycho... I mean cycles anymore.
—D., age 47

I'm not thrilled about it. I mean I will be psyched as hell not to ruin every pair of underpants I own, but I thought I might have kids one day. —L., age 40

life have
er. The
age 48

Not to be melodramatic, but my period and I have known each other for a long time and have been through a lot together. I feel like I'm being asked to say goodbye. And I don't really want to. —J., age 42

In your next life, come back as a man. —S., age 48

Menopause is gonna suck, if my PMS right now is any indication. —E., age 42

Not worried about it. Not worried about anything. I'm really just not worried. —L., age 48

I've a
it's ev

My ass is down to my kneecaps. —S., age 48

Unfertile ground...Mother Earth generates no more...not even having a choice in the matter. (Remember the first flutter?) —D., age 47

As with any
passing of

I wanted to have a baby so badly. I can't believe I'm actually going to leave this planet without experiencing the biggest miracle of all. —S., age 46

I've been infertile for years, so you'd think menopause wouldn't be a big deal, but in fact it feels even more ominous. While you're infertile, there is always this hope of a miracle, of a surprise. But menopause seems to take that hope—however small—away from you once and for all. —J., age 42

As for being infe
Martin Luther Kin
last. Free at last.

What do I think of it? Nothing positive. Gray hair, sagging skin, hot flashes, mood swings. And those are the good days...If I didn't know so many other women in similar straits, I'd think I was going insane. —T., age 55

And speaking of hair...gray pubic hair????? Shut up. —D., age 48

d easily but n o. —D., age 4

mourn the y. —K., age

Menopause is part of life, and if I'm blessed enough to go through it, I should at least try to savor it, learn from it, and not race through it like it's the 50-yard dash. —J., age 42

I am trying to find peace with how my body's going to dry up. The thought of vaginal dryness is awful. I'm having too much fun to be interrupted. Oh well, I guess there's always help in a tube. —J., age 48

up at 58

An older woman, whether meno-pausal or beyond, is 100% woman. The outward appearance changes, not the inner being. —A., age 58

When I was younger, I thought menopause would be a loooooooong time away. Now that it's over, it seems a loooooooong time ago. —S., age 58

People who don't miss being younger are lying. —R., age 51

I don't miss the crap about being young and naive and all the boy crap. —D., age 3

I think, perhaps, that a youthful body is compensation for the underestimated fears, ignorance, and confusion of youth. I'll take psychic peace over a youthful body anytime. —K., age 50

I've lost the ability to get out of speeding tickets. —L., age 42

don't miss being young. I want
focus on the positive side of
owing. —P., age 41

Do I miss being younger? Yes...
I still can't believe that I'm not
35...I was a minute ago...
—S., age 46

No withering!
—A., age 58

I miss wondering what I'm
going to do with my life. I miss
my jeans with the patches all
over them. —E., age 42

I miss my thinness and smooth
springy skin with nary a dimple
except where they're cute. I miss
riding my bike all over the place
just to look at things. I miss
learning things and being really
excited about it. I guess I miss
being eleven. —R., age 51

I feel pretty anchored in my age
and prefer to roll with it than
try and perpetually restore a
younger me...You know what age
scares me? 19. —L., age 47

We are so lost in youth. God, if
I see one more set of fake tits,
I'm going to scream...Why does
society always have to see women
as young, fake, sexualized body
parts? —J., age 48

Are you sure
I'm not bein
graded on t
—R., age 51

Kegels,
kegels,

When I see my wrinkles I'm surprised and think, "Wait, this must be someone else's mirror." I wish I could take the high road on this one, but I never feel as old as I look, and I hate that. —T., age 56

I would never do anything to alter my face or my wrinkles. I've never worn masks, and I wouldn't want to start now. —P., age 41

I want to get sex
and more and mor
with each year. Bu
as good as I can
care of myself...no
—S., age 46

For those who define themselves by physical appearance, aging is a series of assaults. But I think it's an opportunity to get beyond the scramble for sexual recognition and move on to a more integrated humanity. —K., age 50

I saw Tina Turner on the Today Show this morning, and she is sexy and beautiful and smart and talented and CRAZY. If I can be that way at almost-70, then ROCK on. —L., age 40

I admire any woman who has the balls to pose nude in her 60's. —D., age 47

When you were your
STAND UP and have
wall is a nice mem

Dewiness. Gone. You can't help but notice every time you put on makeup that things just don't look the way they used to...all the smiling and pulling your hair back in a tight ponytail can't change the facts. —D., age 47

I wish I could pull my face u̲ from the neck and pin it tig̲ behind the hairline. I don't think that a sagging face is badge of honor, and I may ̲ have to do something about of these days. —A., age 68

xier

o look

̲g

̲nife.

of my grandmother ̲at sticks in my mind is the ̲ightly worried tilt of her ̲ebrows. Sometimes when I ̲ss a mirror I am struck by the ̲semblance. I would never ̲tox my grandmother away. ̲., age 42

I search the crowd for women who seem to be growing old grace-fully, making silent deals that if I can look/act/feel like they do then that's okay. —J., age 42

Stop worryin̲ what's going ̲ in 10, 20, 30 and start doi̲ your exercise̲ —S., age 58

̲could ̲gainst the ̲age 58

Who has the metabolism of a 20-year old? Now we really have to work for that which we had for free...I have to admit that the Ab King Pro on TV is starting to look mighty good to me. —D., age 47

I think my children, grand-children, lover (husband), and friends will love to see my wrinkled face. I hope it speaks of my love of life. —J., age 48

This is what life and fate are about. —D., age 39

It's my responsibility to make of my life what I want. Nobody—not even God if I'm a good girl—will do it for me. —A., age 72

veryone thinks that lder" means "people older than me." But who are 80 have the to think that people 90 are "old people." —S., age 58

I get older, I'd like to push e envelope, help folks bust eir joy seams, and widen their pacity for beauty. —D., age 42

It would be nice to find some kind of meaningful relationship other than that with canines. —D., age 48

Younger men fa —C., age 54

With age, I have gained an almost painful realization of the beauty of life and of those people who mean the most to me. —J., age 42

I don't want to think about having gained or lost. I prefer to think that we transform ourselves, that we reach higher levels of being. —P., age 41

Wisd a ma

older women that I admire
m to be old and young at
e. They are excited by what
oing on, about how the world
hanging, and they are still
oing to make what's new, not
watching. —L., age 42

I'm 72 now, feel wonderful most
days, excited, and am amazed
every time I pass another birth-
day. —A., age 72

More courage, an
less shame. —K.,

with me.

Appreciate yourself. And if you
are blessed to live to menopause,
appreciate the composite (which
every year contributed to) that
you are. —C., age 54

. Experience is
. —D., age 48

It's like a secret that will never
be told—that older women are the
coolest subset of the species.
—T., age 56

I am free to love, and ur
to love and to be loved
in ways that I did not wh
I was younger. —A., age

You must have COURAGE in order to survive. You have it in you, and you have to discover it. Then do what you feel most called to do. —A., age 72

The only cure is to learn to embrace change. —K., age 50

If in doubt, smile, stand up straight, suck in your gut, and try to look like you've just had great sex. —J., age 42

You cannot know where you are
going until you know where you
have been. —D., age 47

Carry on, as they say.
—M., age 49

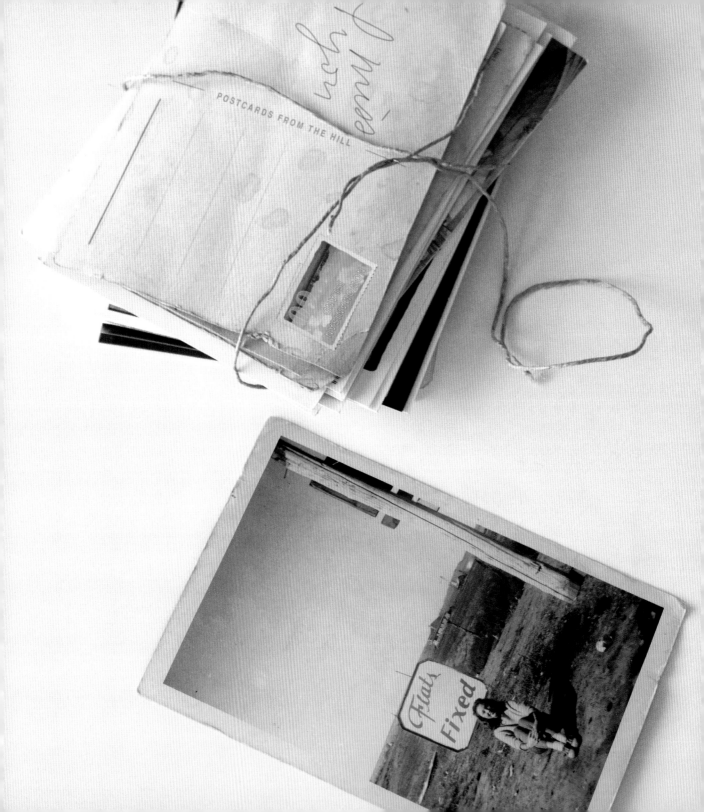

POSTCARDS FROM THE HILL

Flats Fixed

CHAPTER 10
POSTCARDS FROM THE HILL

Wish you were here. The view is beautiful.

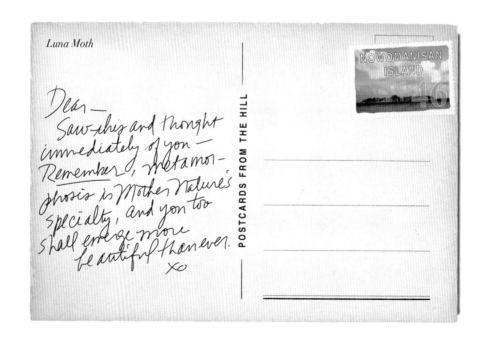

Luna Moth

NOWOMANISAN ISLAND 46

POSTCARDS FROM THE HILL

Dear —
Saw this and thought immediately of you — Remember, metamorphosis is Mother Nature's specialty, and you too shall emerge more beautiful than ever.
xo

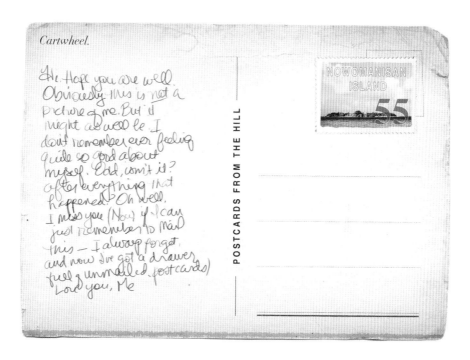

Cartwheel.

Hi. Hope you are well.
Obviously this is not a
picture of me. But it
might as well be. I
don't remember ever feeling
quite so good about
myself. Odd, isn't it?
After everything that
happened. Oh well.
I miss you (Now if I can
just remember to mail
this — I always forget,
and now I've got a drawer
full of unmailed postcards)
Love you, Me

POSTCARDS FROM THE HILL

NOWOMANISAN ISLAND

55

Postcard: *Rarely seen image of the Invisible Woman.*

Note reads: *Look. If we're so invisible, then we can get away with anything. Here's to our crimes of the century. x, Me*

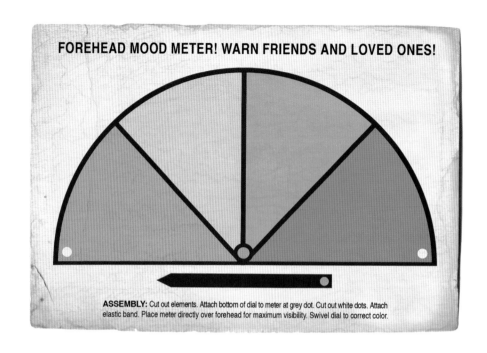

FOREHEAD MOOD METER! WARN FRIENDS AND LOVED ONES!

ASSEMBLY: Cut out elements. Attach bottom of dial to meter at grey dot. Cut out white dots. Attach elastic band. Place meter directly over forehead for maximum visibility. Swivel dial to correct color.

Forehead Mood Meter
Allows the wearer to inform friends and loved ones of current mood.

POSTCARDS FROM THE HILL

MAY YOU BE
FOREVER
GREEN.
♡

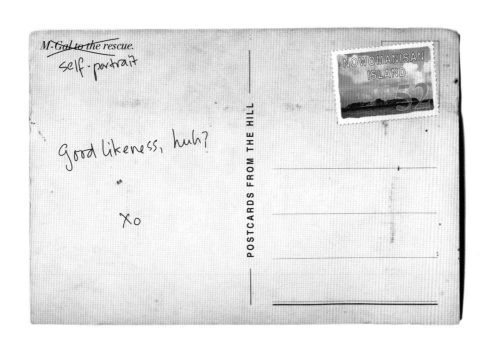

Postcard: *Under Construction*

Note reads: *Every time I think I'm finished, I see that I'm still a work under construction. Always preparing to unveil a new wing, a renovated interior, fixing that place where my roof used to leak. Send paint. Yours, Me*

*this is the life

This is the life. ... and girl don't let anyone tell you otherwise. This life, this age — it's all a gift!

All my love,
C

POSTCARDS FROM THE HILL

NOWOMANISAN ISLAND
60

[NOTE: GROWING OLD IS NOT AN ASSAULT ON HUMANITY

It's not deserving of a prison term. It's not shameful, disgraceful, wrong. Growing older is the gravy, the bonus points, the sign that we lasted when others unfortunately fell.

Maybe all this ludicrous propaganda about age and how we shrink and become less is just a cover-up for the reality that we actually become more. Why else would human beings so desperately hang on if age is such a tragedy? What's old anyway? Isn't any age that's above ours old until we get there? Don't we keep pushing that number higher and higher until the last final gasp? And then in the end we find this: We don't grow Old at all. We just grow Up.]

CHAPTER 11
LETTING GO
(NOT A EULOGY, BUT A WAKE)

Sometimes it's best to go ahead and mourn.

To open up the gates and let the floods come, or the trickle, whatever's waiting to break out. Sometimes we need to open our eyes and admit we're losing things we'll never get back again. That every beginning exists because there is an ending alongside.

We say that menopause is natural, normal, human. As if saying those words makes it easy, painless, effortless.

Which are words we think no one should use.

This change of our lives is a loss we shouldn't trivialize. And lamentations are sometimes needed, if not utterly required.

If we feel sad, let's be sad. If we want to grieve, let's grieve. Some of the things we've lost are gone forever; there will be no replacing them. But even grief has an expiration date.

So say good-bye to the girl you were and the things she didn't get. Say good-bye to the babies you didn't have. The loves that didn't materialize. The hopes you carried around so gently but just couldn't quite, somehow, bring to life.

Mourn the people you've lost; they have no substitute. Mourn the smothered chances, the stillborn dreams; they have a habit of haunting unless you let them go. And then turn the page. And get on with the rest of your life.

CHAPTER 12
ARE WE THE WOMEN WE WANTED TO BE?

You'd watch your mother get ready at the mirror and the murmur in your head went I want to smell like her look like her be like her. You'd wear her scarves and her necklaces, high heels that would slip instead of saunter, you'd paint on her lipstick (the person playing the role of The Mother will be me) and imagine who you would someday be. And you could almost catch her in the right light.

WHEN YOU GREW UP, you would do great things. Conquer the world. Capture kingdoms and hearts, cure animals of all sicknesses, be brilliant and beautiful equally, easily. Fall in love carelessly and often. Never be held down.

You would grow up. But you would not grow old.

And as the years passed you moved through phases and ages, shedding temporary personas if they didn't fit, adjusting others so you looked the part. Sometimes you'd stop and check your progression like some internal growth-chart drawn on an inside wall; sometimes you'd pull out the Map of Your Life to measure how far you'd come, how much distance left to go.

Now you stand with a mile marker at one side and a question bouncing over your head: Am I the person I hoped I would be?

Would the girl I was be proud of the woman I've become? And if not, is it too late to get there?

Whoever you are, and whatever life has flung your way, you have endured. And persevered. You have lived a life equal parts fantasy and reality, the gift of knowing what you want and the compromise of taking what you get. We are all, every one of us, saturated with our experiences, built of them. And as much as we sometimes feel we're carved in stone (or made of salt) we're really made of clay. Not fixed. Not frozen. Not our minds, not our souls, not our selves.

There is still time (years, months, decades) to keep on choosing paths, changing direction. Was there something you were desperate to do (learn, travel, write, teach, create, discover) that for one reason or another never came to be? Is there something still inside howling to get out? Then let it out. There is no one keeping it back except you. Society may shut us out and try to negate our dreams, but the only ones who can truly crush them, obliterate them, are us. We give up because it seems so hard. We

give up because we're not sure we're any good. But there comes a time when we see that the rhythm of our lives is played by us, not the great universal "them." The world and all its gravity knocks us around. We all fall; some of us learn to bounce.

And then there's this: Whatever it is we're intent on "becoming," we're not going to become any of it if our body isn't along for the ride. The preciousness, the fragility, of our bones and our skin and our blood should be apparent to each one of us by now. If we abuse the one-time-only-no-returns-no-exchanges clause our flesh is tagged with, it won't come out with the wash. Our genetics are beyond our control. Everything else is entirely up for grabs.

Despite any evidence to the contrary, we are vital, obstinate, alive, refusing to go away or fade into someone else's distance. We're not now and never will be invisible. If they pretend they can't see us, we'll just have to be a hell of a lot louder. And a hell of a lot more unwilling to fade. Women don't have a shorter shelf life than men; we just have a fuller shelf. The lines on our faces and hands are just as distinguished as theirs, just as dignified, just as reeking of character. Live with them or change them—that's up to you.

Acknowledge your body as your own, give yourself a break, reach for the beautiful thing, the challenging thing.

And that supposedly dreaded phrase "A woman who has really lived"? Maybe we shouldn't dread it at all. Maybe what we should do is embrace it. Wear it like a badge of honor, a prize we get for exhausting all our possibilities and then conjuring up an abundance of more. All that time waiting to become the women we wanted to be, and we're here. We're a harvest, ready to be picked and savored and enjoyed. We're utterly, brilliantly

RI

CHAPTER 13
WOMAN, EXPRESS THYSELF

This book, this paper, this binding, it's all yours. So forget the archaic rules against defacing printed matter, take pen in hand, and go. Write something. Draw something. Create a shamelessly hedonistic haiku. Blank pages just beg to be filled in. And these pages are for you.

What do you think when you hear the word "menopause"? If you've gone through menopause, *how did that whole thing feel to you? If you haven't gone through menopause, how do you feel about entering that next wild frontier? Do you know what menopause will be like? Will it be (or is it) a relief or a curse, this end-of-periods-forever-end-of-laying-eggs-forever-goodbye-*

most-of-my-estrogen thing? What have you lost in getting older? What have you gained in getting older? How does the idea of being infertile for the rest of your life make you feel?

Do you miss being younger? Please explain. (Drawings and sexually explicit limericks are always welcome.) Someone we know described going through menopause like this: "Drying

SELF PORTRAIT/POLITICAL STATEMENT/SELF-CONGRATULATION/ENRAGED DOODLE/ETC.

up and withering away like an old leaf." What say you to that? What is our society not getting _about older women? About older human beings in general? Now: wrinkles. Would you do any-_

thing to get rid of them — seriously? Or do they make you feel like you've lived exquisitely? What's the biggest change that's happened to you since you turned 40? Since you turned 50? Is there a number—an age, a digit—that scares or scared you above all others? Since the average life-

span of first world females is now 82, what do you want to get out of the next decades of your life? When you think about an older woman you admire, what is it about her that you admire _most? What is she like? If you could stand on a soapbox and address the crowd, what would_ *you say? What banner would you wave?*

We couldn't agree with you more.

—J. and C., ages 45 and 43

LAST THINGS LAST

For more advice and information:

bellaonline.com

breastcancer.org

drnorthrup.com

drweil.com

ivillage.com

medicinenet.com

menopause.org

nethealthbook.com

plannedparenthood.org

project-aware.org

truehealth.org

webmd.com

whatreallyworks.co.uk

womenshealth.about.com